MY SLEEPYTIME BIBLE

written by Jan Godfrey | illustrated by Paula Doherty

Tyndale House Publishers, Inc.,
Carol Stream, Illinois

TYNDALE KIDS

Contents

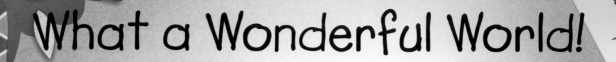

What a Wonderful World!

What a wonderful world our great God made long, long ago!

"Let there be light," said God. And there was!

"Let there be rivers, mountains, and seas; leaves, flowers, and trees," said God. And there were!

Then God made the sun, moon, and stars; wet, slippery fishes; colorful birds; and dainty butterflies. God made animals with swishy tails and tickly whiskers. Some made growly noises, and some made no sound at all.

Last of all, God made people to look after his wonderful world.

"The world I've made is really, really good," said God.

And then God rested—long, long ago.

The Very Bad Snake

Adam and Eve lived in God's beautiful Garden. A very bad and tricky snake lived there too.

"Hiss," said the snake. "Look at that yummy fruit tree over there."

"But God told us NOT to eat from that tree," said Adam and Eve.

"Go on," hissed the snake softly. "This fruit is good for you. It will make you clever and wise."

Mmm—it looked so juicy and tasty. They disobeyed God and took a bite. Then Adam and Eve felt very ashamed and tried to hide. But God knew what they had done. He sent them away from the Garden. And the very bad snake slithered off in the dust.

Noah's Floating Zoo

"It's going to rain—a lot," God said to a good man named Noah. "The people I made have been bad and unkind. But I promise I will keep you safe. Build an ark for your family and all the animals."

Noah obeyed, and his family and all the animals went into the ark, two by two by two by two.

And then it rained and rained and RAINED! The floods came higher and higher. The ark bobbed safely on the water.

At last the rain stopped, and slowly, slowly the land became dry once more. The ark rested on dry land, and a wonderful, shining rainbow appeared.

"I always keep my promises," said God.

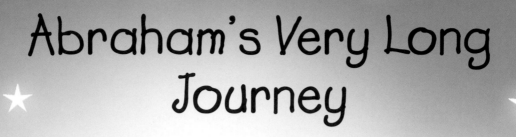

Abraham's Very Long Journey

Many years later, God spoke to a man named Abraham.

"You and your wife, Sarah, must travel to the faraway land of Canaan. I will look after you and bless you."

One dark night in Canaan, God said to Abraham, "Look at all those zillions of stars! One day you will have a son, and then there will be zillions more families—I promise."

One day, three messengers from God appeared.

"This time next year Sarah will have a baby," the visitors said.

"I'm far too old!" laughed Sarah. But baby Isaac was born the next year, just as God had promised.

Very Different Brothers

Esau and Jacob were Isaac's twin sons.

Esau liked hunting wild animals. Jacob liked cooking them.

Esau would lead the family one day. But Jacob wanted to be the leader too!

Isaac grew to be very old, and his eyes couldn't see very well. So Jacob played a trick on him. He brought Isaac a bowl of delicious stew—and dressed up as Esau!

"Here you are, Father," said Jacob.

"Is it really you, Esau?" asked old Isaac.

"Of course," Jacob lied. "Don't I feel like Esau? Don't I smell like Esau?"

"God bless you, my son. You will lead my family when I am gone," said Isaac.

When Esau found out, he was furious!

Joseph, the Favorite Son

When he was older, Jacob had children of his own: twelve sons and a daughter.

Jacob liked Joseph best of all and gave him a special coat. His brothers were very jealous.

Then Joseph had dreams—dreams where all his brothers bowed down to him. And Joseph told his brothers about his dreams. His brothers were furious!

"Who does Joseph think he is?" they muttered and grumbled. "He thinks he's so important—let's get rid of him."

The brothers waited for the right moment, and then they threw Joseph into a pit. They told their dad that Joseph was dead. Jacob was very, very sad.

God Takes Care of Joseph

Joseph's brothers sold him to be a slave far away in Egypt. But God did not forget Joseph.

One night the king of Egypt dreamed strange dreams about grain and cows. Joseph helped him understand what the dreams meant.

"We must save lots of grain," said Joseph, "to stop us

16

from being hungry when the crops don't grow."

The king put Joseph in charge of saving up the grain, which was a very important job.

When Joseph's brothers came to Egypt to buy grain, they didn't recognize their little brother. But Joseph recognized them.

"I know you wanted to hurt me," he told them. "But God was taking care of all of us by bringing us to Egypt where there is plenty to eat."

The Princess and the Baby

"Waaaahhhh!" cried little baby Moses.

"Shh," said his mother anxiously. "The cruel king and his soldiers might hear you. He doesn't like baby boys. They might grow big and fight him someday!"

"Waaaahhhh!" cried baby Moses again.

His mother thought hard. She wove a watertight basket for Moses and hid him beside the river. Moses' big sister, Miriam, kept watch.

After a time, the king's daughter came to take a bath.

"Oh! A baby!" said the princess. "I will look after him."

"You'll need a nurse," giggled Miriam. She ran and fetched her mother—baby Moses' own mother!

God had kept baby Moses safe.

Plagues in Egypt

Moses grew up to be a wise leader who loved God.

One day, God spoke to Moses from a holy, burning bush.

"Tell the cruel king to let my people, the Israelites, go free," said God.

Moses went to see the king, but the king said, "NO!"

Then some horrible things happened. The rivers dried up, leaving yucky mud and frogs and flies. People and animals got sick. Huge hailstones fell from the sky. Clouds of insects ate all the crops.

"Now will you let my people go?" Moses asked the king.

"Oh!" said the king. "Just GO AWAY!"

At last, Moses led God's people safely out of Egypt.

The Big, Wide Sea

God used a fiery cloud to lead Moses and the Israelites out of Egypt. At last they all reached the Red Sea. "It's deep and wide and really scary!" everyone said.

God helped them cross the water. Moses raised his hand over the sea, and the wind blew the waves out of the way. All the people crossed the dry path safely.

Then God looked after everyone. There was special food called manna to eat. There was refreshing water from a rock to drink.

Then one day, Moses talked with God on top of a smoking mountain. God gave Moses ten special rules to help people follow God and live together happily.

Samuel Listens

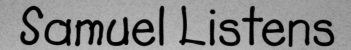

Hannah loved little baby Samuel very much. She knew that God had special plans for him.

When little Samuel was old enough, Hannah took him to the place of worship where the old priest, Eli, looked after him.

One night Samuel woke up.

"Samuel!" called a voice. He went to Eli.

"I didn't call you," said Eli.

Then Samuel heard the voice again. He went to Eli.

"I didn't call you," said Eli.

Then Samuel heard his name again. This time Eli knew that God had spoken to Samuel.

Samuel always listened to God after that. Hannah was right. God did have special plans for him.

God Sees Our Hearts

Seven of Jesse's sons stood in front of Samuel. They were all tall and strong.

"You must choose the next king," God said to Samuel, "one who is truly good and wise inside his heart."

It was hard to choose!

"Is it this one?" said Samuel. "Or that one?"

"No, not this one," said God. "Not that one."

"Do you have more sons?" Samuel asked Jesse. David, Jesse's youngest son, came in from the fields.

"David is good and wise inside his heart," said God. "Choose him."

Samuel sprinkled David with olive oil as a special sign that he would be king and that God would always be with him.

David and Goliath

Goliath was fierce and bad and a GIANT of a man!

One day, King Saul's soldiers watched Goliath coming closer, and they shivered and quivered and quaked!

"I'll fight him," said David bravely. "God has helped me to fight lions and bears. He'll help me now."

"YOU? Fight ME?" roared Goliath. "You're only a boy! And you're not even wearing the right armor!"

"But I come in God's name," said David.

He took five pebbles from a stream and whirled one of them around in a sling. WHAM!

Goliath toppled to the ground—and all his soldiers ran away.

The Friendly Ravens

"It won't rain for a long, long time," said Elijah to bad King Ahab. "God says so. The crops won't grow. You wait and see."

Bad King Ahab thought hard about that.

The rain stopped, just as God had said it would. God told Elijah to go and hide by a little stream.

"You'll have drinking water there," said God, "and ravens will bring you food."

So Elijah obeyed God. He drank from the little stream, and every morning and every evening, friendly ravens brought him food, just as God had said.

God looked after Elijah until the rain fell again on the earth.

Jonah Runs Away

God told Jonah to go to a city called Nineveh, where people did bad, wrong things. But Jonah didn't want to go there! He tried to sail to Tarshish instead.

A huge storm blew up. Jonah knew why.

"I've disobeyed God," Jonah told the sailors. "Throw me into the sea!"

God sent a very large fish to swallow Jonah, and he stayed inside the fish for three days. It was dark and scary!

"I'm sorry," Jonah said to God.

Then—WHOOOOSSSHH!—the big fish spat Jonah onto dry land.

"I promise I'll go to Nineveh now," Jonah said to God. And he did.

33

Daniel and the Lions

Far away in Babylon and far away from home, Daniel worked for the king but worshiped God.

The king's men didn't like Daniel.

"We worship YOU, oh King!" they said. "Send Daniel to the lions because he worships God instead!"

The king didn't sleep well that night. He dreamed about Daniel and those hungry lions. GGGRRRR!

Early next morning, the king went to the lions' den.

"Good morning, oh King," said Daniel. "Look—God has taken care of me!"

The lions padded about softly. The king couldn't believe his eyes.

"Your God really is the true and living God!" said the king.

Mary and the Angel

One ordinary day, a girl named Mary had a very big surprise. God's angel Gabriel appeared right in front of her! Mary felt really afraid and trembly.

"I have a message for you from God," said the angel gently. "You are going to have a baby—the Son of God himself. He will be named Jesus."

This was scary! But Mary was so happy. She was going to
be the mother of God's Son! She ran excitedly to tell her cousin
Elizabeth, and they praised God together.

"You're a great and wonderful God," sang Mary, "yet you still
care about me."

A Baby Named Jesus

One dark night, Mary's baby son was born in a stable.

"God's Son is born in Bethlehem!" angels sang to shepherds, who hurried to Bethlehem.

There, as promised, was a stable, and in the stable stood a manger filled with hay. And in the hay there lay God's Son, the newborn baby Jesus! Wow!

The shepherds knelt and worshiped the baby.
"God's angels sang to us," they told Mary and Joseph.
Mary listened quietly to their story. Then the shepherds went
back to their fields, praising God all the way home.

Following the Star

Far away, some wise and clever men saw a special star high in the sky.

"This is a sign from God," one man said.

"A newborn king," another man said.

"We must find him and bring him gifts," they said.

The wise men traveled for many days, following the big, bright star that was high in the sky. At last the star led them to Mary and Joseph and the baby Jesus.

The wise men knelt down and worshiped the baby. They gave him special presents: gold and frankincense and myrrh. These were very special gifts for a very special baby king—God's Son.

John the Baptist

John lived in the desert. He wore rough, hairy clothes. He ate insects and wild honey. He told people all about God.

"Be ready for God's Kingdom," said John. "Be sorry for all the wrong things you've done. Be kind and fair and good. Someone very special is coming soon!"

Many people were baptized in the nearby Jordan River. Then Jesus asked John to baptize him, too!

"But you are very special—you should be baptizing me!" said John.

"This is what God wants," said Jesus.

As Jesus came out of the water, God's Spirit came out of the sky like a dove.

"This is Jesus, my Son," said God.

Very Special Friends

One day, Jesus sat in a boat on the seashore and taught the people all about God. His fishermen friends were washing their nets.

"Take the nets out farther and deeper," Jesus said to Peter.

"But we haven't caught anything ALL NIGHT!" said Peter.

"Go on," said Jesus.

So they tried again and brought in a HUGE catch of fish. The net nearly broke! Peter couldn't believe his eyes.

"Come with me, and we'll catch more than fish together," said Jesus. "We'll tell people all about God and how to be happy."

And that's exactly what they did.

God Loves You

"Do you want to be really, truly happy?" Jesus asked. "If you search for God, you'll find him. If you're sad, God will give you a great big hug. If you feel really small, you'll discover that God is really big. If you do whatever God asks, you'll feel pleased inside. If you're kind to others, God will be kind to you. If you're truthful, you'll see God. If you try to bring peace, you'll be his children. If you're teased for loving God, then laugh and sing and dance for joy.

"Enjoy being God's friend, and love him," said Jesus. "God loves you a lot!"

The Hole in the Roof

Four friends carried a man on a mattress to find Jesus. The man couldn't walk.

"The house is too crowded!" said one.

"We'll never get near Jesus!" said another.

"What will we do?" asked another.

But the fourth friend said, "I have an idea. Let's make a hole in the roof!"

They cut out a hole, then they gently lowered their friend to Jesus.

Jesus smiled. Then he spoke to the man: "God will forgive anything you've done wrong. Now pick up your mattress and go home."

And to everyone's amazement, the man was healed. He picked up his mattress and went home!

The Very Scary Storm

One calm, quiet evening, Jesus and his friends sailed across the lake. It was so calm that Jesus fell asleep in the boat. Suddenly a wind blew, and the little splashy waves grew higher . . . and HIGHER. The little boat tossed up and down, up and down. Suddenly it was a very scary storm!

50

Jesus' friends were terrified.

"Wake up! Help us! We're going to drown!" they shouted.

Jesus stood up in the boat.

"Be quiet!" he said to the wind and waves.

Right away the storm died down, and the lake was calm and peaceful again.

"Even the weather does what Jesus tells it to do!" said Jesus' friends. They were amazed.

Jairus Needs Help

One day a man named Jairus came running to Jesus.

"Please come quickly!" said Jairus. "My little daughter is very, very sick!"

They set off to Jairus's house, but people crowded around Jesus and interrupted at every step. Jairus grew more and more impatient. His daughter might die!

At the house there was the sound of wailing and crying. They were too late!

"Shh," said Jesus, and he went into the house. "She's only asleep. Come on, little girl, get up."

Jesus took her hand and helped her to her feet.

"She'll be hungry," said Jesus. "She needs something to eat."

Her parents were very, very happy.

Bread and Fish

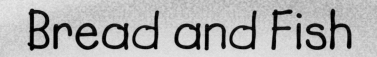

People had been listening to Jesus all day—and they were hungry!

The crowd had grown bigger ... and bigger ... and bigger. Everyone wanted to hear Jesus telling them wonderful things about God.

There was nowhere to buy food, but then a little boy shared his picnic.

"Here you are," he said to Jesus and his friends. In his hands were five little bread rolls and two little fish.

"Thank you," said Jesus. "Thank you, God."

Jesus' friends shared the food—and there was enough for EVERYONE!

It was a VERY big and special picnic!

Stories Jesus Told

Jesus told all sorts of wonderful stories about all sorts of ordinary things: lamps and lights, gates and doors, salt and serpents, bread and birds, camels and coins, thistles and thorns, sheep and shepherds, flowers and seeds and tangly weeds.

Some people listened carefully to what Jesus had to say. His stories were fun! They made people laugh.

"God wants you to love him and love each other," said
Jesus. "Care about other people, share with them, and
forgive them."

Jesus told people that God loved them like a shepherd
loves his sheep. He will search high and low until he has found
even one that is lost.

How to Pray

Jesus told a story about a Pharisee and a tax collector, who were both praying in the Temple.

"I'm glad I'm such a good man," the Pharisee boasted loudly, beaming up at God. "Thank you that I'm not greedy or dishonest like that tax collector over there!"

The tax collector was sad about the wrong things he'd done. "I'm really sorry, God, that I've done bad things," he whispered, hiding his face. "Please, please forgive me."

Jesus said, "The tax collector knew he wasn't very good. But he was really, truly sorry, so God forgave him. The Pharisee wasn't very good either—he just thought he was! Be like the tax collector when you pray to God."

The Man Who Couldn't See

Bartimaeus was a blind man who couldn't see anything at all. He begged by the road for money.

One day Bartimaeus heard Jesus coming along the road.

"Jesus! Make me well!" he shouted.

"Shh," everyone said.

"Jesus! Help me!" shouted Bartimaeus more loudly.

Some kind friends brought Bartimaeus to Jesus.

"What do you want me to do?" asked Jesus.

"I want to see things," said Bartimaeus.

"You will," promised Jesus, and suddenly Bartimaeus could see!
He saw the sky and trees and people—and he saw Jesus.

"Off you go," said Jesus with a smile. But Bartimaeus followed
after him all along the road.

The Man Who Climbed a Tree

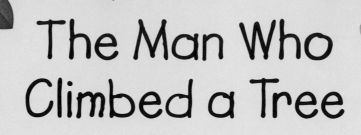

Nobody liked little Zacchaeus very much. He was a rich tax collector and a cheat.

Today, Jesus was coming! Zacchaeus wanted to see him. He ran ahead of the crowds and climbed up into a leafy tree.

Just as Zacchaeus peered DOWN through the branches, Jesus stopped and looked UP!

"Come down, Zacchaeus," said Jesus. "Let's have a meal together."

Zacchaeus happily scrambled down from the tree.

Later on, after supper, Zacchaeus promised he'd never cheat again.

"I'll give some money to poor people too," said Zacchaeus.

"I've come to find people like Zacchaeus," said Jesus, "to help them be God's friends."

Riding on a Donkey

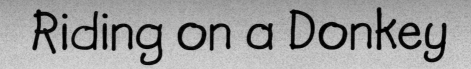

Jesus was riding on a donkey, traveling with his friends to Jerusalem.

Crowds of people followed him along the road, men and women and children, happy and excited people. They were all shouting and cheering.

Jesus was coming!

"Hooray!" they shouted. "Hooray for Jesus!"

The crowd grew bigger and bigger, noisier and noisier. People threw down their coats in front of Jesus and waved palm branches. They pushed and jostled to see the parade.

They shouted and cheered, "Hosanna! Praise King Jesus!"

A few men stood at the edge of the noisy crowd, frowning and not happy at all. They started making plans to get rid of Jesus.

65

One Last Lesson

Jesus and his friends were about to have dinner together. They were hot and tired from walking on the dusty road.

Jesus poured some water into a bowl and tied a towel around his waist. Then he began to wash his friends' feet and dry them with the towel.

"You shouldn't be washing my feet!" said Peter in surprise. "They're all dirty and dusty! A servant should wash them."

"If you're my friend, you'll let me wash your feet, Peter,"
said Jesus. "I've come to love and serve you. That's God's
way—we all need to love and serve one another."

One Last Meal

Jesus and his friends ate lamb and herbs and bread and had wine to drink for dinner.

"Remember me every time you eat bread and drink wine together," Jesus said to his friends. But Jesus knew something bad was about to happen. "Soon one of you will give me away to my enemies," he said.

His disciples shook their heads.

"I would never do such a thing!" said Peter.

"Wait till you hear the rooster, Peter," said Jesus. "You will have said three times that you don't even know me."

Jesus shared some bread with Judas, but Judas would not even look at his friend Jesus. Instead, he got up and silently slipped away into the dark night.

Praying in the Garden

After dinner, Jesus' friends went with him to a quiet, dark garden nearby.

Jesus was sad. He prayed to God.

"Please help me, Father God," said Jesus. "I'm very troubled and very sad, but I'll do whatever you want me to do."

Meanwhile, Jesus' friends fell asleep one by one.

"Couldn't you stay awake with me for a little while?" asked Jesus sadly.

Suddenly his friends woke up! There were noisy, angry voices. There were clattering swords and spears and bright torches coming into the garden. And there was Judas, leading the soldiers to Jesus to take him to his enemies.

Are You Jesus' Friend?

The soldiers took Jesus away to the high priest's house. Peter and John quietly followed them in the darkness and waited outside.

"You know that man, don't you?" a servant girl asked Peter.

"No!" said Peter, scared.

"You're his friend, aren't you?" asked a man.

"No! No! I don't know him!" said Peter again.

"You do know him, don't you?" said some others, coming closer.

"No! No! NO!" lied Peter, really frightened. "I'm telling you—I don't know Jesus!"

Then dawn came—and the sound of a rooster:

"Cock-a-doodle-doo!"

Peter felt so sad and ashamed that he cried and cried.

Carrying the Cross

Jesus was taken away to be crucified. His enemies teased him and hurt him and mocked him. They pushed a crown of thorns onto his head.

"There you are, King Jesus," they taunted. "Now you can carry your own cross."

The cross was big and heavy. Jesus was so tired that he tripped and stumbled. Then the soldiers made a man named Simon carry Jesus' cross up the hill.

The cruel soldiers laughed and shouted. Then they nailed Jesus to the cross.

"Please forgive them," Jesus said to God. "They don't know what they're doing."

Then the midday sky grew dark, the birds stopped singing, and Jesus died.

A Cold, Dark Cave

Some of Jesus' friends carried his body to a beautiful garden.

"Jesus can rest here in my garden among the trees and flowers," said a kind friend named Joseph.

Jesus was buried in a cool, dark cave, quiet and still. Then his friends rolled a huge, heavy stone door across the entrance to the cave.

Nobody could possibly get into the cave—ever! Nobody could possibly get out of the cave—ever!

"Jesus will rest here safely," said his friends. They thought they would never see Jesus again. The world felt still and quiet and sad.

The Stone That Rolled Away

Early on that Sunday morning, Jesus' friend Mary went with some of the other women to the cave where he was buried. They were crying. They were very sad.

But then they saw that the huge, heavy stone had been rolled away. Jesus' tomb was empty! Two shining angels stood there.

"Jesus must be alive again!" they said.

Mary's friends ran to tell Peter and John. But Mary stayed by the empty tomb.

"Don't cry," said a voice. Mary thought it was the gardener.

But then she saw that it was Jesus! Jesus was alive again!

The birds sang happily in the beautiful Easter garden.

"Hallelujah! Jesus is alive!"

79

Thomas Meets Jesus

Jesus really was alive again. He walked and talked with a lot of his friends.

But Thomas had not been there. Thomas just couldn't believe what his friends told him. How could Jesus be dead and then alive? He wanted to see for himself.

He made sure he was there with his friends the next time Jesus appeared.

"Peace be with you," said Jesus, coming into the room one day.

"Look at my hands and feet," he said to Thomas. "Look where the soldiers hurt me. Look at me and touch me. I really am me!"

"You really are you!" gasped Thomas. "You really are Jesus, and you are alive!"

Breakfast by the Sea

Peter and his friends went fishing all night on the Sea of Galilee. But they didn't catch any fish at all. They were tired and disappointed.

Then, just as the sun was rising, they heard a voice from the water's edge.

"Put your nets out on the other side of the boat!"
Suddenly the net was full of fish—big and small, slippery
and wet and wriggly.

"It's Jesus!" the friends shouted—and there was Jesus on the
shore, cooking fish.

"Breakfast is ready!" said Jesus.

"You are my friend," Jesus told Peter. "I know I can trust you
to take care of the others."

Now Peter knew that Jesus had forgiven him.

Brave and Happy People

Jesus promised that the Holy Spirit would come. Now the Spirit had come, and Peter and his friends knew that God was always there to help them. They weren't afraid of their enemies anymore. They were excited and happy and brave and kind.

"Jesus is alive!" Peter said to large crowds of people. Soon those people learned to believe and trust Jesus too.

The believers became known as Christians. They shared their money, clothes, and food, and God helped them heal people who were sick. They prayed together. Every day, more and more people became God's friends.

"God makes us all so happy!" they said.

At the Beautiful Gate

One day Peter and John went to the Temple to pray.

At the busy gate, a man who couldn't walk begged everyone for money.

"Please . . . ," said the man to Peter and John.

"I don't have any money," said Peter. "But I have something better—Jesus has made you well! Get up and walk!"

Right away the man began to feel stronger. He could stand! He could stand and walk! He could stand and walk and *jump!* He could stand and walk and *jump* and *run!* He could stand and walk and *jump* and *run* and *leap* and praise God!

Everyone watched in amazement.

Escape by Moonlight

King Herod didn't like Peter and his friends talking about Jesus. He chained Peter up in prison.

Peter's friends prayed together, asking God to help him.

Peter was fast asleep, guarded by soldiers, when suddenly an angel appeared and woke him.

"Follow me!" said the angel.

The guards didn't notice the chains fall away from Peter. They didn't see the heavy iron gates swing open.

Peter was free! He hurried along the dark street to find his friends.

Knock, knock, knock! Rat-a-tat-tat!

At last someone answered the door.

"It's Peter!" said his friends. "God has answered our prayers!"

89

Saul Learns to Love Jesus

A man named Saul was trying to follow God—but he hated Jesus.

He set out for Damascus, where he hoped Jesus' friends would all be killed or put in prison. Suddenly the road was filled with dazzling light. Saul fell to the ground.

"Why do you hate me?" asked a voice. Saul knew that it was Jesus. "Trust me—there is so much work for you to do."

Saul stopped hating Jesus and learned to trust him. He became one of Jesus' best friends.

Saul spent the rest of his life traveling and telling people about how they could love God and be Jesus' friends too. As he traveled, Saul became known as Paul.

Visit Tyndale's website for kids at www.tyndale.com/kids.

TYNDALE is a registered trademark of Tyndale House Publishers, Inc.

The Tyndale Kids logo is a trademark of Tyndale House Publishers, Inc.

My Sleepytime Bible

Publishing Director: Annette Reynolds

Art Director: Gerald Rogers

Pre-production Manager: Krystyna Kowalska Hewitt

Production Manager: John Laister

Cover designed by Jacqueline L. Nuñez

For manufacturing information regarding this product, please call
1-800-323-9400.

Library of Congress Cataloging-in-Publication Data

Godfrey, Jan, author.

   My sleepytime Bible / written by Jan Godfrey ; illustrated
by Paula Doherty.

     pages cm

   Audience: Ages 2-7.

   ISBN 978-1-4143-9868-6 (hc)

1. Bible stories, English—Juvenile literature. 2. Children—
Religious life—Juvenile literature. I. Doherty, Paula,
illustrator. II. Title.

   BS551.3.G628 2015

   220.95'05—dc23   2014043281

Printed in Singapore

21	20	19	18	17	16	15
7	6	5	4	3	2	1